The Guggenheim Museum Bilbao

TRANSFORMING A CITY

Georgene Poulakidas

Children's Press®
A Division of Scholastic Inc.
New York / Toronto / London / Auckland / Sydney
Mexico City / New Delhi / Hong Kong
Danbury, Connecticut

Book Design: Erica Clendening and Michelle Innes
Contributing Editor: Eric Fein

Photo Credits: cover © Joel W. Rogers/Corbis; pp. 4, 9, 16-17, 22, 36
© AP/Wide World Photos; p. 6 © Jean Gaumy/Magnum Photos; pp. 10, 11,
18, 26, 28 Courtesy of Gehry Partners, LLP; pp. 12, 39 AFP/Getty Images;
pp. 14-15, 34-35 © Yann Arthus-Bertrand/Corbis; p. 21 Agencia EFE; p. 30
Txema Fernandez/Agencia EFE; p. 33 © Pavlovsky, Jacques/Corbis Sygma;
pp. 40-41 © Jose Fuste Raga/Corbis.

Library of Congress Cataloging-in-Publication Data

Poulakidas, Georgene.
  The Guggenheim Museum Bilbao : transforming a city / Georgene
Poulakidas.
  p. cm. — (Architectural wonders)
  Includes index.
  Summary: Chronicles the building of the modern art museum in Bilbao,
Spain, describing how Frank Gehry and his architectural team overcame
many design and construction obstacles, and examines how this
"breathtaking architectural wonder" revitalized an old industrial city.
  ISBN 0-516-24078-1 (lib. bdg.) — ISBN 0-516-25907-5 (pbk.)
  1. Museo Guggenheim Bilbao—Juvenile literature. 2. Frank O. Gehry
and Associates—Juvenile literature. 3. Bilbao (Spain)—Buildings,
structures, etc.—Juvenile literature. [1. Guggenheim Museum Bilbao. 2.
Frank O. Gehry and Associates. 3. Bilbao (Spain)] I. Title. II. Series.

  N3412.4.P68 2004
  727'.7'094663—dc22
                                                              2003015418

1 2 3 4 5 6 7 8 9 10 R 13 12 11 10 09 08 07 06 05 04

Contents

Introduction

Every day, visitors to the Guggenheim Museum Bilbao are greeted by the sight of the giant plant sculpture, called *Puppy*. The sculpture is 32 feet (10 meters) tall. *Puppy* was created by Jeff Koons.

As you walk toward the huge museum, you are filled with amazement and excitement. This structure truly is a wonder of design and construction. Its metal and glass gleams and sparkles in the bright sunshine.

As you approach the entrance, you see a huge sculpture of a dog. When you get closer, you see that it's made entirely out of plants! Once inside the museum, you look around. There is a large atrium, or courtyard, that contains enclosed glass elevators and stairs. The museum's walls are white, with honey-colored stone and green glass. You stand there in awe, thinking: *How did this architectural wonder come to be? How was the Guggenheim Museum Bilbao* (bil-**bah**-oh) *created? How did the port city of Bilbao, Spain, turn itself into a cultural center of the world?*

The idea to revitalize the city of Bilbao by constructing a cultural center such as a museum began in the 1980s. By the early 1990s, the project had gained worldwide attention. The people in charge of the project had a simple yet grand goal: to create a museum that was both a breathtaking architectural wonder and a place to showcase some of the world's greatest art. Creating the museum would be hard work. It would require many people to work together as a team. In the process, Bilbao would be transformed from a forgotten industrial city to one of the world's leading cultural centers.

chapter one

Choosing the Museum Site

Bilbao in Decline

Bilbao is the largest city on the north coast of Spain. It is about 62 miles (100 kilometers) from France. The area Bilbao is located in is also known as Basque country. Bilbao was once a leading industrial city in Spain. Steelmaking and shipbuilding were its two main industries. At one time, Bilbao had the highest income per person of any city or region in Spain. In the 1980s and early 1990s, however, Bilbao suffered economically. There was a worldwide decline in the steelmaking, shipbuilding, and manufacturing industries. Many large industrial companies in Bilbao closed. The result was high unemployment, as well as ruined areas of the city and the Nervión River. In fact, the nearby Nervión River was heavily polluted from all the years that industrial waste had been dumped into it.

Bilbao had also suffered from terrorist attacks for many years. There are people in Basque country who feel strongly that the area should be independent of Spain. Some of these people, called Basque separatists, have committed acts of violence to force the

Years of economic hardship took its toll on the city of Bilbao. Also, factories and other industrial businesses gave off toxic wastes that made the city dirty and grim.

BUILDING BLOCKS

The city of Bilbao is over 700 years old. It was founded by Diego Lopez de Haro in 1300.

government of Spain to agree to their terms. Since 1968, about 800 people have died due to terrorist acts and the related fighting between the Basque separatists and the Spanish government.

The Process Begins

In 1987, the Strategic Plan for the Revitalization of the Bilbao Metropolitan Region was established. The Basque Public Authority, the region's governing body, wanted to bring a modern art museum to Bilbao. They hoped to revitalize the city by doing this. The authority had been looking for a place to build a new museum. They also wanted an organization willing to work with them to design and pay for the construction of a museum.

In February of 1991, the Basque authority reached out to the Solomon R. Guggenheim Foundation. The Guggenheim is an organization dedicated to collecting and showing modern contemporary art in different cities in the world such as New York City and Berlin, Germany. It had been looking for places to build new branches of the

This 1945 photograph shows Solomon R. Guggenheim (right) looking over a model for the planned Guggenheim Museum in New York City. The museum was designed by the great American architect Frank Lloyd Wright (left). Baroness Hilla Rebay (center) was an art advisor to Guggenheim. The New York City Guggenheim opened in 1959.

Guggenheim. The director of the Guggenheim Museum was Thomas Krens. Krens and the foundation were eager to work with the city of Bilbao.

Originally, the Basque Public Authority was planning to turn an old wine storage warehouse, called the Alhóndiga, into the place to show contemporary art. However, the building was in bad shape.

In April 1991, Thomas Krens went to Bilbao for the first time. He took a good look at the Alhóndiga.

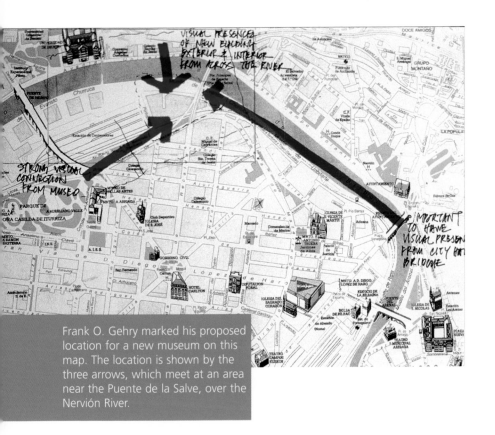

The handwritten notes on the map read: "VISUAL PRESENCE OF NEW BUILDING EXTERIOR & INTERIOR FROM ACROSS THE RIVER", "STRONG VISUAL CONNECTION FROM MUSEO", and "IMPORTANT TO HAVE VISUAL PRESENCE FROM CITY AND BRIDGE".

Frank O. Gehry marked his proposed location for a new museum on this map. The location is shown by the three arrows, which meet at an area near the Puente de la Salve, over the Nervión River.

He did not think it was a good place for a museum. Krens believed a museum must have a large space to display art collections. He thought that the Alhóndiga's inside space was too small and the ceilings were too low. The movement to create an art museum in Bilbao had run into its first problem.

Enter Frank O. Gehry

Even though Krens did not approve of the Alhóndiga as the new museum location, he did not want to give up on the project. He decided he needed another opinion.

This photo shows the area Gehry marked on the map on page 10. The long arrow on the right of the page 10 map is indicating the Puente de la Salve bridge. The bridge can be seen in this photograph.

Krens asked the famous Los Angeles-based architect, Frank O. Gehry, to come to Bilbao. Gehry was well known for transforming industrial spaces into architectural works of art. Krens knew that Gehry would be able to determine if the run-down Alhóndiga could be successfully transformed into a museum.

In May 1991, Gehry went to Bilbao to look over the Alhóndiga. He immediately agreed with Krens that the old warehouse would not work well as a museum. His advice was to build a new museum close to the Nervión River. The site that he liked had

a factory and a parking lot on it. A bridge, the Puente de la Salve, also crossed the site. This bridge is one of six that links different areas of Bilbao that are separated by the Nervión River. This riverfront area included a museum, a university, and an opera house.

Krens and Gehry told the Basque Public Authority that Alhóndiga was not going to work as the new museum site. Eventually, the Basque authority came to agree that the riverfront would be a more exciting place for the new museum. The new site of the Guggenheim Bilbao was finally decided. It would be on the Nervión River, between the Puente de la Salve and Puente de Deusto bridges. After this decision had been made, the next step was to figure out how the new museum would fit into its surroundings. This job would be up to the architect chosen to design the new museum building.

Thomas Krens (left) and Frank O. Gehry (right) worked hard to make the Guggenheim Museum Bilbao a reality.

And the Winner Is . . .

A group was formed to find the best architect and design for the new museum. The group was called the Executive Committee of the Guggenheim Bilbao. The committee was looking for a building with a strong and

unique identity. They wanted people visiting this new museum to not only enjoy the art on display, but also see the building itself as a piece of art. Several architects were invited to take part in the design competition. The architects visited the new museum site in July 1991. Then they started to sketch their designs for the museum.

Frank O. Gehry was chosen as the museum's architect in late July 1991. He understood the committee's goal of creating an exciting building that would redefine the old industrial port of Bilbao. He

Gehry honored Bilbao's history as an industrial port city by working the Puente de la Salve into his design for the museum.

was also sensitive to the new museum's surroundings. He addressed the city's pressing issues, such as how to include the huge Puente de la Salve that occupied most of the new site. Gehry worked the bridge into his design by having part of the museum built under it! Gehry believed that his design would honor Bilbao's history as an industrial port city, while signaling that Bilbao had become a modern twenty-first century city.

History of Guggenheim Museum

Solomon R. Guggenheim began collecting art in the 1920s. In 1939, he opened the Museum of Non-Objective Painting in New York City to exhibit his art collection. This museum was owned and run by the Guggenheim Foundation. In 1952, it was renamed the Solomon R. Guggenheim Museum. It moved to its permanent and current home, also in New York City, in 1959. Other Guggenheim museums have since followed. In 1979, the Peggy Guggenheim Collection opened in Venice. In 1997, the Guggenheim Museum Bilbao opened, as well as the Deutsche Guggenheim Berlin. In 2001, the Guggenheim Hermitage Museum opened in Las Vegas, Nevada. Looking to the future, there will be a new Guggenheim Museum New York in Lower Manhattan designed by Frank O. Gehry.

UM

chapter two

A Challenging Design

Gehry's First Sketches

Gehry focused his museum design on working with the empty riverfront location and the city's business area. According to the city's plans to redevelop Bilbao, the riverfront area was going to be changed into an area of parks, apartment buildings, and shopping areas. However, Gehry did not want to lose the industrial feeling of the riverfront. He planned for a big public area, a water garden, and, of course, the new museum.

Gehry quickly put his first thoughts about the design on paper. This helped create his blueprint for the future development of the project. After Gehry finished his first sketches of the new museum, they were given to the project designer. This person was in charge of building a model based on Gehry's pencil drawings. During the entire design process, many revised sketches and models had to be made.

The New Museum

Gehry's design for the museum called for a building that would be laid out as a series of connected blocks. The museum

Frank O. Gehry made many sketches while trying to come up with a design for the museum that he was happy with.

BUILDING BLOCKS

Frank O. Gehry loves playing ice hockey. In fact, he considers drawing to be skating across paper.

would be made up of nineteen galleries located on three floors. The biggest gallery is more than 430 feet (131 m) long. This is bigger than a football field. This gallery would be used to exhibit huge sculptures. Some people refer to this gallery as the "boat." The museum was also planned to have an auditorium, a restaurant, a library, a gift shop, offices, and a tower.

The smaller galleries all branch out from the large central atrium. This causes the building to take on many different appearances from the outside. From one angle, it looks like a gigantic modern sculpture. From a different angle, it looks like a rose with unfolding petals.

People coming from one of the main city streets are led directly to the museum's entrance. Visitors take a wide flight of steps down into the museum. This is different than most other museum designs, where people have to climb steps to enter the building. There is a low entrance leading to the central atrium that is 15 stories high. This atrium is criss-crossed by catwalks. It has enclosed glass elevators and stairs that bend at seemingly impossible angles. The inside of the building is white with honey-colored stone and green glass.

The Bilbao's main gallery is home to many unusual pieces of art. The curved sculpture shown in the middle is called *Snake*. It was created by Richard Serra.

Gehry's design offers a series of eye-opening experiences. In the smaller galleries, you are able to look outdoors, beyond the works of art on display. Most architects focus on creating ways for visitors to best appreciate the art in the museum. However, Gehry takes visitors further. He joined the architecture of the building and the art displayed on the walls. For example, when you enter a gallery, you may see a painting on a wall. You might then glance to the side and catch a glimpse of the street through an oddly shaped window. The scene of the street may look exactly like the painting on the wall. Without being aware of it, the visitor is led to compare the painting on the wall and the framed street scene.

Tensions Build

Gehry's original design for the Guggenheim Bilbao called for it to have a tower. The tower became the subject of disagreement. The tower was to be built on the other side of the Puente de la Salve.

Gehry's design for the museum's tower (to the right of the museum) was not set until the late fall of 1994. Gehry originally considered making the tower out of glass. He also considered making it out of a mix of limestone and metal. However, these ideas were rejected.

It did not have a function. However, there was limited money left in the construction budget. The lack of money meant that the tower could not have more than one flight of stairs leading up to the deck level of the bridge. Gehry wanted to postpone the construction of the tower. He did not want to go over the $100 million budget. To further stay under budget, he wanted to use plaster instead of limestone for the offices that would be inside the museum. These offices were to be used by the museum's staff and some of the galleries. However, Gehry's suggestions were not well received by the Basque Public Authority. They insisted that Gehry use stone as the office material and not plaster. They also thought the tower needed to stay part of the building. So, the tower was developed as a connected part of the building.

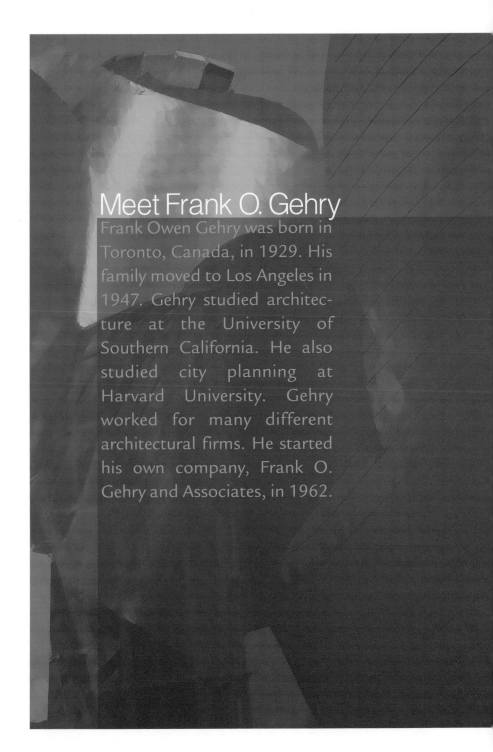

Meet Frank O. Gehry

Frank Owen Gehry was born in Toronto, Canada, in 1929. His family moved to Los Angeles in 1947. Gehry studied architecture at the University of Southern California. He also studied city planning at Harvard University. Gehry worked for many different architectural firms. He started his own company, Frank O. Gehry and Associates, in 1962.

chapter three

From Vision to Reality

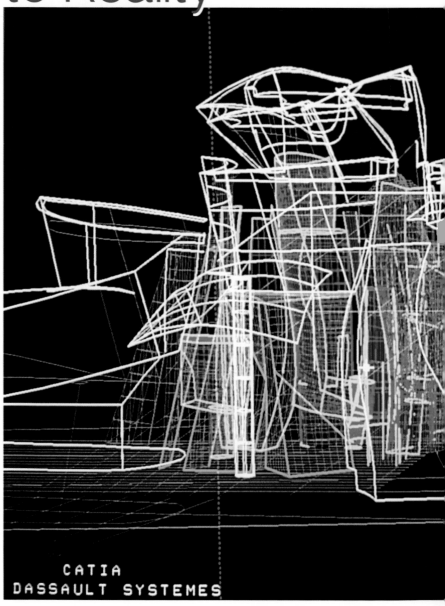

CATIA
DASSAULT SYSTEMES

More Than Drawings

To help design the museum, Gehry and his staff used computers and a special computer software program. The computer software was called Computer-Assisted Three-Dimensional Interactive Application (CATIA).

CATIA made things easy for Gehry, who does not like to use computers. First, Gehry drew his designs by hand. Then he built paper and cardboard models of them. Gehry's workers took over and began transforming his drawings and models into computer graphics. The new Guggenheim Bilbao is one of the largest projects designed with the help of this 3-D modeling software.

How CATIA Works

Once a hand-built model had been created, it was scanned into CATIA using a 3-D scanning machine. More mathematically accurate models were then made. This technology gave Gehry more freedom with his designs and provided him with important information about the museum's construction. For example, specific

Pictured is a computer drawing of the Guggenheim Museum Bilbao. Computers played an important role in the planning of the museum. However, Gehry was reluctant at first to allow them to be used. He was concerned using a computer would limit his design options.

This model shows how the museum would fit into its physical surroundings. On the left, the Puente de la Salve bridge and the museum's tower can be seen.

information could be generated on how to best cut the stones for the building. This helped control the costs of the project. In fact, despite Gehry's concerns about the cost of the tower and building materials, the museum was finished under its $100 million budget.

Finding the Right Exterior

Originally, lead copper was to be used in the construction of the museum. However, lead copper was outlawed as a toxic material. The museum's planners had to find another material. Gehry and the planners wanted materials that could interact with

The skin of the museum is made of thin titanium panels. Here, workers clean each panel by hand.

light the way lead copper did. This led to a long, frustrating search. Gehry and his staff first looked at stainless steel. However, they did not like the cold industrial look of it. Then they considered using titanium. Titanium is a very strong, silvery gray metal. By looking at it in the light, the museum's planners realized that the titanium had the warmth and character that they were looking for. However, titanium was much more expensive than steel. It was also not certain if titanium would be workable for this project.

Titanium had rarely been used as an exterior, or outside, material for buildings. It was mostly used in making airplane parts, golf clubs, and other objects in which strength was needed. Gehry had his staff and the company hired to supply the titanium conduct several tests. After much research

BUILDING BLOCKS

The museum structure is about 256,000 square feet (24,000 square meters). Of this, 118,403.015 square feet (11,000 sq. m) is for exhibiting, or displaying, artwork.

and testing, it was finally decided to use titanium. The panels on the Guggenheim Bilbao are a third of a millimeter thick and cover most of the building. They are guaranteed to last one hundred years.

The titanium panels for the Guggenheim Bilbao were shaped in a factory in Italy. They were then shipped to the construction site in Bilbao. At the site, the workers had to follow strict instructions to install the panels. They had to lay down the panels exactly as defined by the computer. Much of the museum is covered with the titanium panels.

About Titanium

Titanium is thinner than stainless steel. It doesn't lie flat, and a strong wind makes it flutter. This causes it to ripple and make sounds in the wind, giving the impression that the building is "alive" and "breathing." As it reflects sunlight during the different times of the day, the titanium seems to change colors.

Titanium replaced lead copper in the museum's construction. Lead copper had been outlawed as an unsafe material.

Building the Museum

Once the designs were approved and the building materials decided upon, the museum was built very quickly. Construction of the museum started in October 1993 with the knocking down of the industrial buildings that were on the site. This was done so that the foundation could be created. The foundation is the solid structure that a building is built upon. Usually, the site where a building is to be built is dug up and the ground strengthened so that it will

The roof of the museum, with its curving and folded panels, is as much a work of art as anything displayed inside the museum.

hold the weight of the building that will be built on top of it.

The museum's building was made with three layers of steel. The stone used for the building was brought to the construction site and reshaped. It was hand chosen so it would match the other stones that would surround it. Finally, 2,200 glass panels were used for the museum. Of these, 2,000 had unusual and complicated shapes.

chapter four

A City
Transformed

Grand Opening

The museum was finished on October 3, 1997. After the museum was completed, there were about two weeks of events to celebrate the museum's completion. On October 18, 1997, about ten thousand people turned out to watch Spain's King Juan Carlos officially open the museum. He flipped on a switch, which lit up the museum during the evening ceremony. The Guggenheim Museum Bilbao opened to the public on October 19, 1997. It became an instant hit with people all over the world. In its first year, it attracted over 1.3 million visitors—about three times more people than were originally expected!

The Guggenheim Museum Bilbao and Pop Culture

The Guggenheim Museum Bilbao quickly became as popular as some celebrities. Filmmakers, musicians, and even fashion designers wanted their works associated with the museum. It was used as a backdrop during the opening scenes for the James Bond action film, *The World Is Not Enough*. The music group Simple Minds used one of the museum's galleries as a setting for their music video, "Glitter

A big party was held in the museum's atrium to celebrate the official opening of the Guggenheim Museum Bilbao.

Ball." Designers Carolina Herrera and Paco Rabanne used the central atrium as a fashion show catwalk to introduce their new clothing collections.

Building a Better Bilbao

The success of the Guggenheim Museum Bilbao had a major impact on the city of Bilbao. It signaled an upturn in the city's prospects. The Basque Public Authority had also planned other projects to help redevelop Bilbao. All the new projects were held to

BUILDING BLOCKS

Among its art collection, the museum has works by Marc Chagall, Willem De Kooning, Roy Lichtenstein, Pablo Picasso, Robert Rauschenberg, and Andy Warhol.

the high standards of the museum. Sir Norman Foster designed the city's new subway system, the Bilbao Metro. It opened in 1995. World-famous architect Cesar Pelli was asked to develop a river-front project. The project, near the museum, will

Since its opening, the museum has hosted many different events. In 2001, Japanese artist Hiro Yamagata staged a laser light show at the museum.

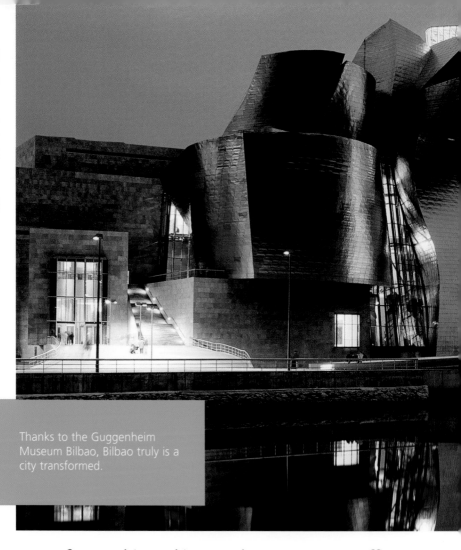

Thanks to the Guggenheim Museum Bilbao, Bilbao truly is a city transformed.

turn a former shipyard into parks, apartments, offices, and shopping areas. Santiago Calatrava designed a new airport for the city. Bilbao also has several other projects in various stages of construction, including a new water-treatment system for the city.

The success of the Guggenheim Museum Bilbao has brought new jobs and money into the area. Tourism has become a major source of income for the city. New hotels and restaurants have been

opened. However, the city and its people have not just benefited economically from the museum's presence. Thanks to the success of the museum and the other projects inspired by it, the citizens of Bilbao now have a positive outlook. They feel good about Bilbao and its place in the world. The Guggenheim Museum Bilbao has brought new life to the city of Bilbao—transforming it for the better!

New Words

architect (**ar**-ki-tekt) someone who designs buildings and checks that they are built properly

architecture (**ar**-ki-tek-chur) the art of designing and building structures

atrium (**ay**-tree-uhm) a patio or courtyard around which a building is built

catwalk (**kat**-wawk) a narrow walk or platform

foundation (foun-**day**-shuhn) a solid structure on which a building is built; also an organization that gives money to worthwhile causes

gallery (**gal**-uh-ree) a place where paintings, sculpture, photographs, etc., are exhibited and sometimes sold

industrial (in-**duhss**-tree-uhl) to do with businesses and factories

New Words

limestone (**lime**-stohn) a hard rock used in building

port (**port**) a town or city with a harbor where ships can dock to load and unload cargo

revitalize (ree-**vie**-tehl-eyes) to give something new life

riverfront (**riv**-ur-fruhnt) any land or area of a city or town that is located beside a river

separatists (**sep**-uh-rah-tihsts) people who want to be separate or a part from another group of people

structure (**struhk**-chur) something that has been built, such as a house, an office building, a bridge, or a dam

terrorist (**ter**-ur-ist) someone who uses violence and threats to frighten people into obeying

For Further Reading

Chollet, Laurence B. *Frank O. Gehry*. New York: Harry N. Abrams, Inc., 2001.

Greenberg, Jan and Sondra Jordan. *Frank O. Gehry: Outside In*. New York: DK Publishing, Inc., 2000.

Van Bruggen, Coosje. *Frank O. Gehry: Guggenheim Museum Bilbao*. New York: The Solomon R. Guggenheim Foundation, 1998.

Resources

Organizations
Guggenheim Museum Bilbao
Abandoibarra Et. 2
48001 Bilbao
Spain
Telephone: (34) 94 435 9080

Solomon R. Guggenheim Museum
1071 Fifth Avenue
New York, NY 10128-0173
Telephone: (212) 423-3500

Resources

Web Sites

Guggenheim Museum Bilbao

www.guggenheim-bilbao.es/idioma.htm

This is the official Web site of the Guggenheim Museum Bilbao. You can learn about the history of the museum, see what is in their collection, and find out what artists will be showcased at the museum.

Guggenheim Museum

www.guggenheim.org/

This is the official Web site of the Guggenheim. It has links to all of its museums in New York, Las Vegas, Venice, Berlin, and of course, Bilbao.

Index

Index

About the Author

Georgene Poulakidas lives in San Francisco, California. She has studied and traveled throughout Spain and loves the Spanish culture. Georgene has taught a first grade Spanish bilingual class in San Francisco for seven years. She now works at an educational toy company in the Bay Area of the city.